# Teach and Test ABC's and More

Reading and Writing Tips for Parents

© 2021 Copyright
by Oksanna Crawley

Note: There is a link to my website for printable worksheets.
For the print book, the printables are available on my website or
they can be photocopied for personal use.

# TABLE OF CONTENTS

LET'S GET STARTED .................................................. 1
THE ABC's ............................................................... 3
   TEACH LETTERS AND SOUNDS ................................. 3
THE ABC's ............................................................. 12
   TEST LETTERS AND SOUNDS ................................. 12
SIGHT WORDS ........................................................ 14
   TEACH SIGHT WORDS ........................................... 14
   TEST SIGHT WORDS .............................................. 18
   SOUNDS AND SYLLABLES ...................................... 19
   GRADE ONE SIGHT WORDS .................................... 21
READING TIPS ....................................................... 22
   READING TO YOUR CHILD ..................................... 22
   HOW TO READ BOOKS TO YOUR CHILD ..................... 25
   HOW BOOKS WORK .............................................. 28
   USING SONGS AND POEMS TO TEACH READING ........... 30
   WHAT TO SAY TO HELP YOUR CHILD READ ................. 34
   THE RIGHT BOOKS ............................................... 40
   HOW TO USE LEVELLED BOOKS .............................. 43
   WHAT TO SAY TO HELP YOUR CHILD READ ................. 47
WRITING TIPS ....................................................... 48
   TEACHING BEGINNING WRITING .............................. 48
   STAGES OF WRITING DEVELOPMENT ........................ 50
   BEGIN TO WRITE ................................................. 53
   WRITING SIGHT WORDS ........................................ 57

| | |
|---|---|
| WRITING LETTERS | 58 |
| WRITING NAMES | 60 |

**RESOURCES** ............................................................. 63
    BOOKS, LINKS, AND MUSIC ..................................... 63

**PRINTABLES** ............................................................ 65
    LINKS AND WORKSHEETS ....................................... 65
    HOMEMADE PLAYDOUGH ....................................... 77

**ACKNOWLEDGEMENTS** ............................................. 78
**BIBLIOGRAPHY** ........................................................ 79
**ABOUT THE AUTHOR** ................................................ 80

## Dedicated To

Parents, who are their child's first teacher

Teachers of literacy

And

To all my students who inspired me everyday

> "You can find magic wherever you look. Sit back and relax all you need is a book!
>
> Dr. Seuss"

# LET'S GET STARTED

Congratulations! You'd like to help your child become a successful reader. You've come to the right place.

I'm a former kindergarten and master reading teacher. I want to share my knowledge with you!

Here you'll find advice on how to teach and test letter names and sounds. You'll learn which sight words to teach, how to pick the right books for beginning readers and which reading prompts to use. Most important of all, you'll learn how to instill a love of reading. This information is for beginning readers and writers.

Reading and writing go hand-in-hand so I'll have tips on beginning writing, too.

> *Reading is a message-getting activity...writing is a message-making activity.*
>
> Marie Clay

## READING AND WRITING...

The better you are at reading, the better you'll be at writing, and vice versa. When a child reads, they are trying to get a message from the print and the picture on the page in front of them. The brain is working hard to make meaning. When a child writes, they are trying to construct a message usually for someone else.

## MAKING SENSE...

What your child reads has to make sense. It helps if there is a story line, even a simple one, to help make meaning. Pictures that support the words in the book are very important for beginning readers.

## PHONICS...

And then there's the matter of phonics. Many parents think this is the way that children learn to read. Not exactly. Yes, it's important to know the letter names and their sounds, but that is only part of how we learn to read. There's a lot more to it! I'll be telling more about that later.

> **Have fun, keep things light and remember to praise your child for successes and just for trying!**
>
> **It's okay to make mistakes— that's how we learn.**

# THE ABC's

## TEACH LETTERS AND SOUNDS

**There are many ways to learn the letters of the alphabet.** Children can watch children's TV programs and play educational computer games. But, I'll show you some simple things you can do at home to teach letter names and sounds. Children often prefer home-made things and it's less expensive! My cell phone was two soup cans and a string!

**Start with lower case or small letters - a, b, c.**
Then add in the upper case or capital letters A, B, C. Why? Take a look at this page. What do you see more of? Upper or lower case letters? Right! Your child will need to know both to read most effectively. Teach your child to write with lower case letters not block or capital letters.

## TEACH LETTERS AND SOUNDS

### Read alphabet books!

- Say the *name* of the letter and say the *sound* it makes. E.g. This is the letter "a". It makes the sound "a" as in "apple".

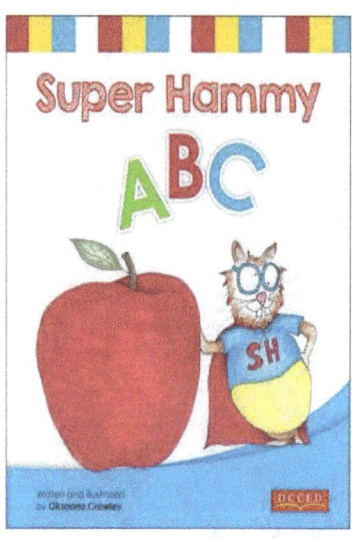

- Find alphabet books at your public library or book store.

- Make friends with the children's books librarian. They can help you find the right books for your child.

- *SUPER HAMMY ABC* teaches both letter names and sounds. (See Resources)

### Teach the alphabet song.

- An oldie but goldie! This is a fun and easy way for your child to learn the letter names.

### Put magnetic letters on your refrigerator door.

- Start with about 3 letters. You don't want to overwhelm your little person with 26 upper case and 26 lower case letters. That's 52 letters!

- Show your child each letter and say its name.

- If your child already knows a letter or two, make sure to include them in a group with one or two new ones. This builds confidence. Say the *sound* the letter makes, too.

TEACH LETTERS AND SOUNDS

## Make your child's name. It's meaningful!

- Use a capital letter for the first letter and lower case letters for the rest of the name. This is how it is taught in school.

- Make the name, leave it there, then ask your child to make it directly under the one you did. Repeat.

- If your child has a very long name, shorten it if possible: Chris for Christopher.

## Scramble the magnetic letters.

- Later, when your child knows several letters, scramble them, and say: Show me 'm'. Show me 'a' and so on.

## Play a matching game with the magnetic letters.

- You'll need two sets of magnetic letters (you can buy them at the dollar store). Put 2 sets of 5 different letters up on the fridge. a, a, b, b, c, c, d, d, e, e

- Scramble them. Show your child how to match the letters.

- Scramble them again. Say: Now, you match them.

## Play with alphabet puzzles.

- Name the letters.

- Say the sound the letter makes.

# TEACH LETTERS AND SOUNDS

- Play a game thinking of words that begin with that sound. Say: Mommy begins with the sound "m". What other words begin with "m"?

## Play with alphabet toys such as blocks or sponge letters.
- Name the letters.
- Say their sounds.
- When teaching the vowels, keep it simple for now. Teach one sound that the letter makes e.g. For the vowel "a", teach the short ă sound as in "apple".

## Play 'What's the Mystery Letter?'
- Once your child has learned some letters, put 5 magnetic letters in a bag or a shoebox with a hole cut in the lid. Decorate the box – make the hole look like a dinosaur mouth. You get the idea!
- Have your child pull one out at a time and name it. What sound does it make? Can you think of a word that begins with that sound?
- Don't forget to praise your child.

## Play with letters in the bath tub.
- Buy some sponge letters.
- Float a few in the tub.
- Ask your child to find and sink different letters one at a time.

## Use soap paints in the bath tub.
- You can write letters on the tiles, or on your child! Or on Mommy or Daddy!

# TEACH LETTERS AND SOUNDS

- Guess the letter!
- Have your child write the letters. Name them. Say their sounds.
- Write your child's name on the tiles. Capital letter first, followed by lower case letters.
- Read it while running your finger under the letters from left to right.

## Make letters out of play dough.
- Roll out the play dough and shape a few letters.
- Have your child run his or her finger over the letter the way you'd print it.
- Give verbal directions while you model how to trace the letter. For a lower case 'a', say: "Around and down, around and down."
- Say the sound the letter makes.

HOMEMADE PLAYDOUGH RECIPE (See Resources)

## Paint letters with water.
- Give your child a bucket of water and a big paint brush and let them 'paint' letters on the driveway.

# TEACH LETTERS AND SOUNDS

- Draw letters in the sand. In the snow.
- Name those letters. Say their sounds.

## Alphabet Fishing Game.

- This is simple and fun and how I taught my own children the alphabet.
- Print the fish template on card stock or thick paper.
- Make 5 copies.

## Print: ABC FISH TEMPLATE (See Resources)

## TEACH LETTERS AND SOUNDS

## Play the Alphabet Fishing Game (continued)...
- You'll need 52 fish.
- Cut out the fish. Print one letter on each fish:
- a capital "A" on one fish, a small "a" on another fish, and so on.
- Attach a paper clip to each fish.
- Make a fishing rod using a small stick (a paintbrush will do, or a dowel from the hardware store). Attach a string with a magnet on the end. It will pick up the paper clip. The small horseshoe magnets are perfect.
- Make it easy. Put only 3 fish on the floor face down so you can't see the letter. Always include letters your child knows. Your child will "catch" a fish, turn it over and tell you the name of it. Do only a few at a time.
- Once a few fish have been collected, have your child match the upper case letter with the lower case letter.
- A variation of the game: Lay out 5 different fish face up. Ask your child to catch a specific letter.
- Another variation: Ask your child to pick out the letter that makes a specific sound.

## Use the books you're reading together to teach letters and sounds.
- After you've read the story, pick a page and point out letters.
- Do one at a time. E.g. Show your child the letter "b".
- Point and say: This is "b". Can you find another "b" on this page?
- Try another letter on another day.

## TEACH LETTERS AND SOUNDS

- Point out both upper and lower case letters.
- You can teach sounds this way, too.
- Point to a "b" at the beginning of a word and say: This letter makes the /b/ sound as in this word "boy".
- Can you find another word that begins with the /b/ sound? Say the word together emphasizing the /b/ sound and pointing to the letter "b".

## Play "I spy…"

- Say: I spy with my little eye something that begins with the sound "m". What is it?

## Make a personal ABC book for your child with your child.

- This is a very useful tool that can stay with your child through to and during grade one!
- The idea is to associate a letter with an object or action that is meaningful to your child. This makes it easier to remember. E.g. D d (draw a dinosaur or dog)
- You can use index cards for this. You'll need 26. Or cut any thicker paper into 5" x 3" cards. Punch a hole in the upper left corner.
- Join together with an "O" ring or a piece of string.
- Print the one letter on each card like this: **A a**
- Use the simple form of each letter, e.g. **a** not *a*, **g** not *g*
- For A a, ask your child for something that begins with the short ă sound
- If it's apple, draw an apple.

## TEACH LETTERS AND SOUNDS

- Associate an action with it if you can – pretend to take a bite of the apple while saying the sound ă.

- Say "a-a-a - apple" while pretending to take a bite of an apple.

- Make a letter card for the sounds your child already knows first, leave blank cards in the stack of 26 and add a letter/sound card each time your child learns a new letter/sound. Review the letters and sounds from time to time.

- This personal ABC Booklet is a handy tool can be used not only for reading but also for writing later on. Keep it close by when reading or writing.

# THE ABC's

## TEST LETTERS AND SOUNDS

Here are two simple tests for letters and sounds.

<table>
<tr><td>

**Letter Names**

Point to each letter starting at A and go across to U. Ask your child to name the letter. Circle the letter if your child knows it.

| A | F | K | P | U |
|---|---|---|---|---|
| B | G | L | Q | V |
| C | H | M | R | W |
| D | I | N | S | X |
| E | J | O | T | Y |
| Z | | | | |

| a | f | k | p | u |
|---|---|---|---|---|
| b | g | l | q | v |
| c | h | m | r | w |
| d | i | n | s | x |
| e | j | o | t | y |
| z | | | | |

</td><td>

**Letter Sounds**

Point to each letter starting at A and go across to U. Ask your child what sound the letter makes. Circle the letter if your child knows the sound.

| A | F | K | P | U |
|---|---|---|---|---|
| B | G | L | Q | V |
| C | H | M | R | W |
| D | I | N | S | X |
| E | J | O | T | Y |
| Z | | | | |

| a | f | k | p | u |
|---|---|---|---|---|
| b | g | l | q | v |
| c | h | m | r | w |
| d | i | n | s | x |
| e | j | o | t | y |

</td></tr>
</table>

You'll have to judge when your child is ready for this assessment. When your child is about 4 years old and you've been teaching the ABC's for several months, you can try this. Make it fun. Do only a part of it at a time if needed.

## Print: LETTER NAMES TEST  (See Resources)

- Place the worksheet in front of your child.
- Using a piece of paper, cover up the letters so that only the top row of letters is showing.
- Ask your child to name the letters beginning with A and going across the page from left to right.
- Circle the letter with a pencil if your child knows it.
- Afterwards, work on the letters your child doesn't know yet.

## TEST LETTERS AND SOUNDS

- Try this assessment in a few weeks to see the gains your child has made.
- Use a different coloured pencil to circle the letters.
- Learning the letters will take time – weeks and months.

## Print: LETTER SOUNDS TEST (See Resources)

- Do the same with this as above.
- Ask your child what sound the letter makes.
- Or, do they know a word that starts with this sound?
- Work on unknown sounds. Praise your child!

# SIGHT WORDS

## TEACH SIGHT WORDS

**What are sight words?** They are the building blocks of beginning reading. They are words such as *it, is, am, and, the, you, I, he, she, here.* It's important to build them up. They are words that your child will be able to recognize on sight, quickly, without actually having to read them. It will speed up the reading process and make things easier. They will be important for writing, too.

This is a list of 30 sight words that children should know by *the end of senior kindergarten* (adapted from Fountas & Pinnell).

| I  | it | he | can | look |
|----|----|----|-----|------|
| a  | to | do | and | here |
| am | is | me | the | said |
| an | no | go | see | like |
| at | so | we | you | come |
| up | in | my | red | down |

Print: KINDERGARTEN SIGHT WORD LIST (See Resources)

## TEACH SIGHT WORDS

## Use the books you're reading to teach sight words.

- When you're starting out, with a child that is about 3 to 4 years old, I'd use the books you're reading with your child as a teaching tool for sight words.

- This way the word is in context in a story not isolated on a flash card. It'll make more sense to your child. You can use flashcards with sight words later.

- After reading a short book, go back to the first page.

- Look for a sight word you'd like to teach, let's say the word "up".

- Read the sentence with the word in it, running your finger *under* the words from left to right, point to the word and say: "That's the word 'up'. Can you find another 'up' on this page?"

- Point out the same sight word at the beginning of a sentence: Up

- Point out it's the same word even though there's a capital letter at the beginning •**Up   up    The   the   This   this    Here   here**

## Use magnetic letters

- Another day, point out the word "up" again.

- This time bring out the magnetic letters - u and p.

- Print the word on a piece of paper, or on a little whiteboard.

- Show your child how to make the word using the magnetic letters directly *under the word you printed*. Say: up.

- Have several sets of the letters "u" and "p" handy.

# TEACH SIGHT WORDS

- Ask your child to make the word at least 3 times *under the word you printed*.
- Have your child say "up" each time."
- Ask: What word did you make? That's right, "up"!
- You'll have to do this several times over many days.
- Ask your child to write the word instead of using magnetic letters in the same manner. Leave your model of the word on the paper or whiteboard for your child to copy. Have them write it 3 to 5 times. Review words every few days.

## Go slowly and build in lots of repetition.
You might have to point out the same word many different times on many different days. That's okay. Introduce a new sight word when your child has demonstrated a firm grasp of the initial one. Review words regularly.

## Point out words in the environment.
There are words all around us. When you're out on the street or in the mall, point them out: Stop. Enter. Exit. Push. Pull. Up. Down. McDonald's. Tim Horton's. Starbucks.

## Sight Word Flashcards.
Use flashcards in addition to teaching sight words by using the books you're reading with your child. But, use the books

## TEACH SIGHT WORDS

first. Remember, we want the words to be meaningful to your child. When you point out a sight word in a story you've read, your child sees how the word is used.

## Print: SIGHT WORD FLASHCARDS (See Resources)

- You can use card stock. Laminate them if you can.
- Once you've introduced a sight word using a book, show your child the flashcard.
- Say the word. Run your finger under the word from left to right while you read it.
- Ask your child to do the same.
- Build up a bank of sight words over days, weeks or months.
- Punch holes in the cards and tie with a string or attach a ring. Review every day.
- For homemade laminating, use clear packing tape to cover the cards front and back.

Image-Carina Fulton

# SIGHT WORDS

## TEST SIGHT WORDS

**These are the sight words that your child should know by the end of kindergarten.** They can't be learned all at once. Before you actually begin teaching your child to read on his or her own, your child might know just a few of these words, maybe only one or two, maybe more, maybe none. That's okay. It depends on the child. Teach as you go. Remember make it fun. Do a little at a time. You want your child to enjoy learning about reading.

Here's a simple test to find out how many sight words your child knows.

## Print: KINDERGARTEN SIGHT WORD TEST (See Resources)

### Kindergarten Sight Word Assessment

Ask your child to read the sight words one column at a time starting with the first column on the left.
Cover up the other columns with a piece of paper.
Circle the word if your child knows it.

| | | | | |
|---|---|---|---|---|
| I | it | he | can | look |
| a | to | do | and | here |
| am | is | me | the | said |
| an | no | go | see | like |
| at | so | we | you | come |
| up | in | my | red | down |

-adapted from Fountas & Pinnell

# SIGHT WORDS

## SOUNDS AND SYLLABLES

**Phonological and Phonemic Awareness.**
These are terms you might hear teachers using. Both are important for both reading and writing.

**Phonemic awareness is** the ability to hear and manipulate individual sounds that letters make.

| cat | k ă t |

There are 3 individual sounds or phonemes in this word.

| weight | w ā t |

There are also 3 individual sounds or phonemes in this word. Don't confuse letters with phonemes.

**Phonological awareness** means being able to also hear and manipulate bigger chunks of sound such as syllables and blends such as bl- , tr-, spr- and digraphs such as ch- and sh- . How to take words apart and put them back together.

The chunks are: -at   - ack.

| hat | h / at |
| black | bl / ack |

## Clap syllables together.

- Start with your child's name. Clap the number of syllables. For example with the name, Larissa, you'd clap 3 times – La-ri-ssa. Do more family names.

# SOUNDS AND SYLLABLES

- Find objects around you, name them and clap the syllables. How many syllables?

## What word am I saying?

- Say the word "cat" stretching out the sounds slowly: **k - ă - t**.
- Ask your child to identify the word.
- Try other simple words: dog, hat, sit, red, up, am, it, he.
- Do some examples for your child. Show them how to do it.
- Try what colour am I saying?

| r - ĕ - d | bl - ue | p - ĭ - nk |

- Try the reverse: Say the word cat. Stretch it out slowly. What sounds can you hear?
- You can stretch an elastic band as you say the word to get across the idea of stretching out word.
- Try chunking the sounds. Say the beginning sound first, followed by the last part or chunk. See if your child can figure out which word you're saying.

## Say: What word am I saying?

| h - at / t - op / c - an |

## Do some examples for your child:

| s - un   is 'sun' |

## Try these words:

| b/at | h/op | c/an | r/un |
|------|------|------|------|
| c/at | t/op | p/an | b/un |
| s/at | m/op | r/an | s/un |

# SIGHT WORDS

## GRADE ONE SIGHT WORDS

PRINT: GRADE ONE SIGHT WORDS (See Resources)

### Grade One Sight Words

| | | | | |
|---|---|---|---|---|
| all | came | how | or | us |
| are | did | if | out | very |
| as | from | into | put | was |
| away | get | little | play | went |
| back | going | make | saw | what |
| be | had | make | she | where |
| because | has | not | that | who |
| been | have | now | they | will |
| but | her | of | this | with |
| by | him | one | two | your |

-Fountas & Pinnell

# READING TIPS

## READING TO YOUR CHILD

**When do you start reading with your child?** The earlier, the better! Babies enjoy touching and looking at books and their wonderful, colourful illustrations. Chewing on them is fun, too. Make it a bedtime routine. At our home, after bath time, we'd cuddle on the bed in our pajamas and read several beloved books over and over again. Children want to hear the same story many, many times and that's great! As long as your child wants to hear it again, keep doing it. They are still getting something out of it.

**Board books are perfect to begin with.** You can show your baby the pictures and read the very simple text while baby is sitting in their little chair or on your lap, or lying on the bed. If you're waiting at the doctor's office, you can keep your little one entertained with some board books. My favourite ones are by Sandra Boynton. To see a list of recommended Picture Books to read with your child, go to **Resources**.

**Have lots of books in the house.** Buy them from children's book stores, second-hand book stores, thrift shops, ask for hand-me-down books from friends and family or take them out of the library for free! Get to know the children's books librarian at your local library. Take your child to free story time at the library. If English is not your first language, you can read books in your mother tongue, too. Your local library has children's books in different languages.

**Model reading behaviour.** Let your children see you reading books or magazines. Show them you value books and reading.

**Expose your child to the language of books.** "What big ears you have!" said Little Red Riding Hood. "Once upon a time..." It's not the same as spoken language. It's not the kind of language we use in casual conversation day to day. It's important to hear the language of books because it'll help your child understand and predict what words might come next when they begin to read.

**Be sensitive to your child's attention span.** When they're very young, infants and toddlers, you might spend only 10 minutes with a book or two. That's okay! You want them to enjoy the time. Don't force it. When they're a bit older, 15 minutes. By the time they're in kindergarten, you'll be able to spend even longer on a book or books, but, each child is different. Go with the flow.

**Use rhymes.** There are lots of wonderful nursery rhymes to say out loud, or read, such jewels as "Jack and Jill", "Little Miss Muffet" and "One, Two, Buckle My Shoe". You can also teach counting with the last one! See **Resources.**

**Use songs.** Put on a CD of songs for children at home or in the car. Some of my favourites are: Raffi, Sharon, Lois and Bram, and Fred Penner. Don't forget the classics such as "Twinkle, Twinkle, Little Star". Sing little ditties such as "Itsy, Bitsy Spider" whenever you can, lunch time, bath time, any time at all. You don't have to be a great singer. Your child is learning new words and sentence structures! Sing songs in your native language if it isn't English. See **Resources.**

**Tell oral stories.** Children love to hear stories about your childhood or their grandparents'. You can use your first language, too, if it's different from English. My parents used to tell me oral stories in Ukrainian. The important thing is to expose your child to the structure of stories. Stories have a beginning, middle and end. They have a setting and different characters.

**Talk to your child!** Talk to your child while doing all the ordinary daily activities such as cooking. "Mommy is stirring the tomato sauce. Now, I'm going to pour it into this bowl.

# READING TO YOUR CHILD

Mmmm, it's going to taste so delicious!" Expose your child to oral language as much as possible. Describe what you're seeing, smelling, tasting, touching. "Look at that beautiful sunset! The colours are lovely. There's orange and pink and yellow!" This is very important! Your child is learning vocabulary and sentence structures. The better your child's oral language skills, the easier learning to read will be. Put down that phone and talk to your child.

**Use the computer but go to the library, too!** Books are available online free through your public library. There are many good literacy games online. But, I still think it's important to have real books in the house and to teach your child to read using real books. Go to the library to get a library card for your child! Let them choose their own books. Get help from the children's librarian. Books with a sentence pattern that repeats, or books that rhyme are excellent for beginning readers. Buy books at your local book store, thrift shops or online. There's nothing like holding a book in your hands. Instead of putting a tablet or phone in your child's hand, give them a book!

# READING TIPS

## HOW TO READ BOOKS TO YOUR CHILD

Read the book all the way through the first time without stopping.

- This lets your child hear the story as a whole, take in the language and helps with comprehension and enjoyment.

Then you can go back and spend a bit of time on each page.

- Point to the objects on the page, and say their name: "Oh, look! That's a cow! A cow says 'moo'."

- With older children, you can go into more detail: "We get milk from a cow."

- But, again, take your cues from your child. Don't belabour it. When my daughter first saw a picture of a cow, she asked "Can it eat you?"

## Shared Reading.

- Use a familiar book that you've read with your child before and share the reading.

- You can read a sentence and leave off the last word for your child to fill in.

- Perhaps your child knows the story by heart. In that case you can take turns reading one page at a time if the book has one sentence to a page. Use your finger to point under each word as you read. It's perfectly okay if your child has memorized the words and is "reading" by heart. This is how reading begins.

When your child is older, in kindergarten or grade one, these are things you can do:

**Before reading:** Look at the cover. Read the title. Talk about what's on the cover. Ask your child to predict what the story might be about by looking at the picture on the cover. Take a picture walk through the book quickly and simply. Don't read it yet. Just look at what's happening in the pictures. You can ask your child: "What's happening here?" You can also name or label some objects in the pictures. "This is a tricycle. That's a vase with pretty flowers."

**During reading:** Once in a while before you turn the page, ask your child to predict what might happen next. If there's a word or vocabulary your child hasn't heard before, explain it. Is this story about reality or is it fantasy?

**After reading:** Talk about the story. " Did you like it? Which part? Was it scary? Which part? Do you remember when you were scared?" Make connections to your child's life and experiences. Compare the story to a similar one or to a different version of the same story such as The Three Little Pigs. What's the same? What's different? Is there a lesson to be learned from this story?

**Retell the story.** You can ask your child to tell you the story! Not read it, tell it. Help out if needed with some prompts. You can also show your child the pictures to aid in retelling. Finger puppets are wonderful to act out the story.

## Ask:

- **Who are the characters?** Ask your child who their favourite character is.
- Who else is in the story?
- **What is the setting of the story?**
- Where does the story take place?
- **What was the problem in the story?**
- How was it solved?
- **What was your favourite part?** Why?

# READING TIPS

## HOW BOOKS WORK

**We need to show children how books *work*.** There are some important features about books, or the print on a page, that you should point out to your child as you read. Teachers call them "concepts about print". Review many times. Focus on one thing at a time. Do it once or twice while reading a book.

## Demonstrate:

- This is how we hold a book.
- This is the front of the book.
- This is the title.
- This is the first part of the story. Point to the first page where the story begins.
- This is the last part of the story. Point to the last page where the story ends.
- This is where we begin to read on a page. Point to the upper left-hand corner and the first letter of the first word.
- This is the way we go. Run your finger from left to right under the words in the first sentence.

- Point out letters. Do one at a time. Show your child the letter 't'. Point and say: This is a 't'. Can you find another 't' on this page? Another one?

- Try another letter on another day. Point out both *upper and lower case letters.*

## For older children (4 years and up):

- **Point to a period.** Say: This dot means stop. We stop reading when we come to it.

- **Point to an exclamation mark - !** This is an excited mark. It means we say the words in an excited way – like "Help!"

- **Point to a question mark - ?** This is a question mark. It means it's asking something "Where's Grandma?"

- **Point to a word in bold or darkened letters.** "STOP!" This means we say it with a big voice.

- Say it.

- **One word.** Ask your child to show you one word. Hug the word – put one finger on either side of it. Show your child the spaces between words. Children don't understand the concept of "word" in print. Count the words in a sentence.

- **One-to-one matching.** While reading, show your child how to use a finger to point under each word as they say it or as you say it. This also helps with the concept of word.

**Print: HOW BOOKS WORK CHECKLIST** to keep handy while reading with your child. (See resources)

# READING TIPS

## USING SONGS AND POEMS TO TEACH READING

Use songs and poems your child already knows to teach reading.

### Matching with Sentence Strips - Using the Happy Birthday Song:

This song is a good one to begin with because chances are your child knows it!

- Hand print the song with a thick black marker onto a piece of white bristol board.
- One sentence per line.
- Leave a space between the lines.
- Now, do this again but this time cut each line individually so that you'll have 4 sentence strips.
- Place the bristol board with the song on a table or the floor.
- Place the sentence strips beside it but mix them up so that they're out of order.
- Demonstrate for your child how to match the sentences.
- Show her how to look for the first word, the last word, words in the middle. Are they the same?
- Place the sentence strip directly under its matching sentence.
- Read or sing the song with your child pointing to each word as you do.

# USING SONGS AND POEMS TO TEACH READING

- Simple! Jumble up the sentences again. Have your child give it a go. Help as needed.
- Read or sing it again.

## Matching with Words - Using the Happy Birthday song:

- This time, your child will be matching the words.
- Make another set of sentence strips just as you did before. Cut the strips into words.
- Place the scrambled words next to the Happy Birthday bristol board.
- Show your child how to match a word or two by placing the word under its match.
- Ask them to match the rest of the words.
- Read or sing the song pointing under each word.
- You can give your child some hints about what to look for when matching a word. Point out the first letter, last letter, letters in the middle, a period

Happy birthday to you.
Happy birthday to you.
Happy birthday to you.
Happy birthday to you.
Happy birthday dear ____.
Happy birthday dear ____.
Happy birthday to you.
Happy birthday to you.

## Work on Sight Words - Using the Happy Birthday song:

- Choose a sight word from the song.
- Use the kindergarten sight word list for reference.
- A good sight word from the Happy Birthday song would be "to" or "you".
- Make the word with magnetic letters on the table or a small whiteboard.
- Have several sets of the letters needed to make the word handy.
- Ask your child to make the word at least 3 times. Say the word each time.
- Ask your child to do the same. "What word did you make? That's right, 'to!'"
- Do one word a day.
- Later, print the sight word on a piece of paper and have your child print it under your word several times
- Use any song or nursery rhyme your child knows such as Twinkle, Twinkle, Little Star or Humpty Dumpty.

## USING SONGS AND POEMS TO TEACH READING

But, your child has to know it by heart in order for this to work.

- Don't forget to have your child point to each word as he or she reads it.

# READING TIPS

## WHAT TO SAY TO HELP YOUR CHILD READ

Learning to read is about more than phonics. Try to sound out these words:

> the = t h eh

> saw = s ah wuh

> tough = t oh you guh h

It doesn't work very well. Instead, children basically use 3 strategies when learning to read. By that I mean when they're trying to figure out the words on the page. They ask themselves:

**Does it make sense?**
**Does it sound right?**
**Does it look right?**

Here's how it works. Let's apply the strategies one at a time to this sentence which you might find in the story, Little Red Riding Hood.

## WHAT TO SAY TO HELP YOUR CHILD READ

"I'm going to _____ you," said the wolf.

## Does it make sense?

- Your child is reading the story and knows that the wolf has gone to Granny's house. They see a picture of the wolf, with an open mouth, standing over Little Red.

- What does the wolf want to do? What would make sense?

- The child reads: I'm going to **eat** you," said the wolf. Does it make sense? Yes.

- The child used the meaning of the story, the context, and the picture to figure out the word. This is why we never cover up the picture.

- This reading strategy is the most powerful one and the one we should use first. Notice that we didn't need any letters (phonics) to figure out the word.

# WHAT TO SAY TO HELP YOUR CHILD READ

## Does it sound right?
This should be: "I'm going to **eat** you," said the wolf.

- Let's say that the child says: "I'm going to **eagle** you," said the wolf.

- Does that **sound** right? Is that how we say things in English? No, it doesn't sound right to our ear because "eagle" is a noun and we need a verb here. It doesn't fit the grammar or syntax of English.

- It's doesn't make **sense** either.

## Does it look right?
This should be: "I'm going to **eat** you," said the wolf.

- Let's say the child says: "I'm going to **kill** you," said the wolf.

- Does that look right? Let's compare. Are the letters there to make those sounds? Is there a "k" at the beginning of the word? No, there's an "e". Is there an "l" at the end? No, there's a "t".

- So, "kill" doesn't look right. It makes **sense** but it doesn't **look** right.

- What word would look right? This one starts with an "e" and ends with a "t". What word would make sense? And sound right? Look at the picture!

- Would "eat" make sense? Yes. Does "eat" sound right - I'm going to eat you. Yes.

- Does it look right? Yes, there's an "e" at the beginning and a "t" at the end.

Our brains use these strategies very quickly. We also use our knowledge of sight words to read more quickly – we don't have to try to figure out those words.

And we can predict what words come next by using the context of the story and our knowledge of English grammar or syntax (oral language).

There you have it! Those are the 3 basic reading strategies. And, as you can see, we often use more than one of those strategies to figure out a word. That's called crosschecking.

You're reading a book with your child who is trying to figure out a word on the page… what do you say to your child?

# # 1 Does it make sense?

Your child is using the story context, the meaning of the story, and the illustration or picture.

This is the most powerful and useful reading strategy that we all use. Use this first. Say:
- **Look at the picture.**
- **What would make sense?**
- **Think about the story.**
- **What would make sense? Try the word.**

# WHAT TO SAY TO HELP YOUR CHILD READ

## # 2 Does it sound right?

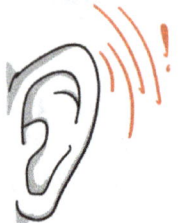

You want your child to use language structure or the way we talk to help her figure out the word. For example: Dog the barks. (It doesn't sound right. We don't say it like that. We say: The dog barks.) Say:

- **Does that sound right?**
- **Can we say it like that?**
- **Do we talk like that?**
- **What could word would sound right and make sense?**

## #3 Does it look right?

You want your child to look at what they *see* on the page – at the letters, at the way the word *looks*.

**Look at how the word begins.**

**What letter do you see?**

**What sound does it make? Go back and read the sentence again and say that first sound.**

Or:

**You said: _____**

**Are all the letters there to make the sounds of the word you just said?**

**Run your finger under the word from left to right saying the sounds to check.**

It would also be natural here to add:
**And does that word make sense here?**
What has been done is called **cross-checking** – using more than one strategy at a time. This is what we want good

## WHAT TO SAY TO HELP YOUR CHILD READ

readers to do – use more than one reading strategy at a time. We do this all the time even as adult readers.

Remember to praise your child even for attempts. You want your child to take a risk and try.

Say: **I like the way you tried to figure out that word.**
Or: **You noticed that something isn't right. Good. Let's figure it out.** (Use the 3 strategies)

If your child can't figure out the word, don't wait too long. Give it to them in 5-10 seconds. We don't want to overwhelm your child. Reading should be fun. And **NEVER** cover up the picture! Your child needs to use it for meaning – to use the first strategy.

Did we say: Sound it out! NO! Do you see how much more powerful and meaningful these 3 strategies are?

We guide our children initially and in time they will use these strategies automatically. Teachers use these strategies or prompts when teaching reading.

**Your child does not have to know all the letters to begin reading!** Why, you may ask? Because we use more than letters and sounds (phonics) when we read.

We use these three different reading strategies:
- **Does it makes sense?**
- **Does it sound right.**
- **Does it look right?**

Even if your child is not reading before they start school, if you've done all of the things I've suggested up to this point, your child will be primed and ready to become a successful reader! And, writer!

# READING TIPS

## THE RIGHT BOOKS

**If you're going to teach your child how to read, you'll need the right books.** Teachers use levelled books. Some systems use letters e.g. A, B, C. Some use numbers e.g. 1, 2, 3. Levelled books make it easier to learn and to teach reading. They increase in complexity gradually and in a highly-controlled way. The vocabulary, sight words, sentence structures are carefully controlled, so is the size of the print, the spacing between the words, the pictures and punctuation. The early books are short.

I've written and illustrated the books below.

### *HERE COMES SUPER HAMMY* - LEVEL 1 OR A

This is what the first two pages look like. There is one sentence on one line. Notice the size of the letters and spaces between the words. The picture supports the print - it provides **meaning** cues for your child. **Never** cover up the pictures!

THE RIGHT BOOKS

## *SUPER HAMMY AND LITTLE MOUSE GO* - LEVEL 2 OR B

A level 2 book has two lines of words. Note the spacing and size of letters, the exclamation mark. The picture supports the print.

## This is a level 3 (C) book.

There are now three sentences on three different lines. We also see quotation marks, not just periods. There's more variety in sentence structures. There can be more than three lines or sentences.

By the end of kindergarten, students should be reading at Level 3 or C.

**Levelled books can be purchased from educational publishers.** I've listed some suppliers in **Resources** at the end of this e-book.

# THE RIGHT BOOKS

The levelled books you see above are part of the: SUPER HAMMY – MY FIRST READING SERIES written and illustrated by me. They are published by DC Canada Education Publishing and are available directly from the publisher or on Amazon. The books can be purchased individually or as a set.

See **Resources** at the end of this e-book.

I've used my experience working with kindergarten and grade one students to produce books which I think children will enjoy reading and which will motivate them. They can read about a goofy hamster super hero named Super Hammy and his misadventures with his buddies – Little Mouse, Bad Cat, Rona Raccoon, Sidney Skunk, Donna Dog, Piper Penguin and Hammy's family. There are 30 books, levels A to F, in both English and French.

# READING TIPS

## HOW TO USE LEVELLED BOOKS

- Picture books are usually read *to* a child.
- Levelled books are used to teach reading to a child.
- In time, it is expected that the child will be able to read the leveled book themselves.

**Always keep the ABC booklet and the sight word flashcards handy while teaching reading.**

## Begin with Level 1 or Level A books.

- You'll need about 5 Level 1 or A books.
- You'll also need a familiar picture book for each day. This is a picture book you have read to your child before. It's used as a warm-up.
- You'll read the levelled books over and over until your child has memorized them. And, that's okay!
- Encourage your child to read along with you or finish the sentences.
- At some point, your child will take the book from you and want to 'read' it to you. This is what you want. It doesn't matter if they've memorized it. Let them use the pictures to jog their memory.
- **Never cover up the pictures!** Pictures are meaning cues.
- This is supposed to be easy and fun for your child.
- Give as much support as your child needs.

## HOW TO USE LEVELLED BOOKS

- **To be clear, we're not expecting the child to actually read the words at this point.** We don't want your child struggling to figure out a word. Tell them what it is if they get stuck.

## This is what you do.

- **With five level 1 books, find a quiet spot .**
- Start by reading a familiar picture book to your child. This is a warm-up.
- Show your child the first levelled book. Say the title.
- Talk about the picture on the cover briefly discussing what the story might be about.
- Read the whole book to your child. Talk about what happened.
- Re-read the book if your child wants you to.
- Read the next four levelled books in the same manner. Re-read them.

## Make the reading sound as natural as you can. Make it sound like you're talking. Read with expression!

- Take your cues from your child as to how much discussion there is about the books.
- Keep the books in a little basket in a safe spot such as on a book shelf.
- Read these same levelled books over and over again for a week or two or longer depending on how old your child is.
- But read a different picture book as a warm up.

HOW TO USE LEVELLED BOOKS

## Now do the same with the Level B or 2 books

- After a week or so of reading the level A or 1 books, introduce the level 2 books.

## How long this process takes depends on your child.

- We want your child to have memorized the books.
- They should be able to "read" the books from memory quickly and easily.
- If more time is needed, repeat this process as many times as needed.
- If it's just not working, give things a break. Your child is likely not ready.
- Keep reading other picture books to your child, and after a few weeks or even months, try again. One day, things will click.

## Move on to Level 3 (C) books.

Once your child has mastered level A (1) and 2 (B) books, move on to level C (3) books and so on.

45

## HOW TO USE LEVELLED BOOKS

When working with level 3 books use the 3 reading strategies:

**Does it make sense?   Does it sound right?   Does it look right?**

- Keep your child's ring of sight words handy. If while reading a level 3 book, your child doesn't recognize a word that you know they know, e.g. *the* show them the sight word on the ring.

- You can also show them the word in one of the level 1 or 2 books they've "read" and know.

Level 3 is a crucial stage and it will take some children longer than others to master. This will take a few weeks or longer depending on your child. A child at the end of kindergarten should be reading at level 3.

Up to this point, we haven't been expecting your child to actually read the level 1 and level 2 books. The books have been memorized. That is perfectly all right at this point. Now, reading really starts to take off.

Your child should have a basic knowledge of how books work, where to start reading, which way to go, that there are letters and words on a page, how to point to words, what a period means, and so on. You will likely have to teach these things again several times. That's perfectly normal.

All of the pre-reading activities I've given you will set your child up for success in reading. Don't worry if your child isn't reading until later in kindergarten. Each child progresses at different rates. Remember reading at level 3 comes at the end of kindergarten.

# READING TIPS

## WHAT TO SAY TO HELP YOUR CHILD READ

## Print: WHAT TO SAY TO HELP YOUR CHILD READ (Resources)

### READING PROMPTS

PROMPTS TO USE WHEN YOUR CHILD IS TRYING TO FIGURE OUT A WORD IN A SENTENCE. START WITH NUMBR 1 OR 2 ALWAYS.

1. LOOK AT THE PICTURE FOR CLUES. WHAT WORD WOULD MAKE SENSE?
2. TRY A WORD THAT MAKES SENSE.
3. TRY A WORD. DOES THAT SOUND RIGHT? DO WE TALK LIKE THAT?
4. TRY A WORD. YOU SAID_____. CHECK THE WORD WITH YOUR FINGER. ARE ALL THE LETTERS THERE FOR THE SOUNDS YOU MADE?
5. SAY THE FIRST SOUND OF THE WORD. WHAT WOULD MAKE SENSE?
6. GO BACK TO THE BEGINNING OF THE SENTENCE, RE-READ AND SAY THE FIRST SOUND OF THE WORD YOU'RE TRYING TO FIGURE OUT? WHAT WOULD MAKE SENSE?
7. RUN YOUR FINGER UNDER THE WORD AND SAY THE SOUNDS SLOWLY. WHAT WORD WOULD MAKE SENSE?
8. IF YOUR CHILD CAN'T FIGURE IT OUT, GIVE IT TO THEM.

PRAISE YOUR CHILD!

# WRITING TIPS

## TEACHING BEGINNING WRITING

### Reading and writing go hand in hand

- What your child learns in reading will help in writing and vice versa.

- That's why they are taught at the same time. It's called balanced literacy.

- While reading, when we ask our child to point under each word as they read it, they're developing an awareness that words are separate things.

- This translates into writing when we ask them to leave a space between the words.

- While writing the word "cat", your child might search for the letter which makes the "k" sound. Whether they discover that it's a "c" on their own or with your help, the next time they're reading a book and they come to a word that begins with that letter, they'll likely remember that it makes a "k" sound.

### Tools for writing

- **Provide an environment which encourages writing.**

- My kindergarten classroom had a writing centre. You can set one up in your home. It can be your kitchen table, or a child-sized table and chair in a corner of a room.

- The writing supplies can be kept in a bin or basket on the table or a nearby shelf. The dollar store is a great place for writing supplies.

- **A variety of things to write with.** Pencils. Fancy pencils. Skinny and chunky markers. Pens. Fancy pens.

## TEACHING BEGINNING WRITING

Crayons. Dry-erase markers. Chalk. Store them in plastic cups, cans, etc.

- **Provide different kinds of paper.** Unlined paper. Big and little paper. Little notepads. Themed paper. Booklets or journals. Recycled paper - use the back. Coloured construction paper. Blank greeting cards. Recycled greeting cards and wrapping paper. Little whiteboards or blackboards.

- **Other useful things.** Erasers. Scissors. Glue. Glitter glue. Tape. A fancy little stapler. A hole-punch. Yarn. Rings for booklets. Little clipboards.

# WRITING TIPS

## STAGES OF WRITING DEVELOPMENT

**Children's writing development goes through some predictable stages.** The age at which the stages occur varies with each child.

### Scribbling Stage

- At this stage, children will enjoy making scribble marks on paper with crayons, markers or maybe even a chunky pencil.

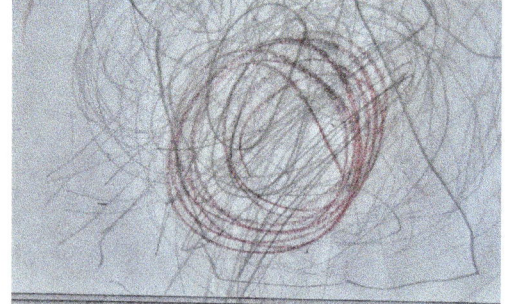

- The scribbles tend to be circular and large and may look like a drawing. Perhaps your child has seen you writing and is imitating you.

- Or, they are simply enjoying the tactile experience of crayon or marker on paper.

- There can be meaning behind scribbles, too.

- The age range can be up to 3 or 4 years of age.

### Letter-like Forms and Strings of Letters

- After a while, some of the marks might resemble letters but they'll be placed randomly on the page along with some scribbles.

- Eventually, your child will know how to form a few letters and will produce strings of random letters.

- This is the beginning of writing from left to right – the way we read.

# STAGES OF WRITING DEVELOPMENT

- There will be no spacing between the letters.

- Drawings will likely accompany letters.

- Your child is starting to get the idea that writing has a message.

- Remember that you've been reading books to your child and they have been looking at letters and words on the pages. They've been watching others write.

## Beginning Sounds of Words

- The child begins to represent a word with the first letter usually a consonant.

- There is an emerging awareness that letters and words are different.

- There may be spacing between the words/letters.

- The child might write a message about a picture he or she has drawn.

- The child can write his or her name.

- This occurs around age 4 or 5. This is perfectly fine!

- Iwtb or I w t b     (I went to bed)

## Final and Middle Sounds of Words

- At this point, the child not only writes the first letter of a word, but also the last letter.

- The last letter is usually a consonant, too. e.g., the word "went" is written as **w t**

51

## STAGES OF WRITING DEVELOPMENT

- Consonants are easier to hear than vowels. There can be spacing between the words. The writing is from left to right. Most of the letters might be capitals.

- The child can produce a simple sentence.

- After, the child becomes aware of the middle sound of a word, a consonant or a vowel.

- This is when invented spelling occurs; the child writes what they hear. Invented spelling is fine! Correct spelling comes later.

- The child can usually write some sight words and the names of siblings, as well as some words in the environment such as 'stop'.

- This occurs around age 5 or 6.

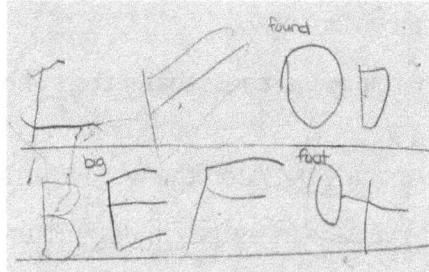

"I found Big Foot"
Stages of writing images:
Mrs. McCabe's Kindergarten class

# WRITING TIPS

## BEGIN TO WRITE

## Writing Letters During Writing

- When your child is in the middle of writing a sentence, and can't remember how to make a letter, practise it.

- Keep a piece of blank paper handy and show your child how to make the letter.

- Use your child's **ABC booklet**.

- Don't forget to use verbal directions, too – down, down and around, and so on.

- By the time you get to the point of trying to write a sentence or story, you should have been working on letters, their sounds and sight words for a while.

## Writing Stories

- A story at this point can be a simple sentence on each page of a little booklet.

- It can be two pages long or a few pages long depending on your child.

- Make a booklet out of unlined, printer paper. Cut the paper in half and staple together a few pages. You can make an "I Can" book with your child.

# BEGIN TO WRITE

- Make a cover. Print "I Can" on it. Have your child write their name and draw a picture of themselves. On each inside page, print: I can_____

- Talk about the different things your child can do - sing, dance, walk, run, skip, catch, throw, ride a bike, etc.

- Have your child draw a picture of what they can do.

- Ask your child to write what they can do using some of the techniques I've described earlier.

- Read the book together. Ask your child to read it to as many people as possible!

- You've created what's called a **"pattern book"**. The structure of each sentence is the same except for the last word. This makes it easy for your child to read.

- You can also make a pattern book using photos you take of your child doing various activities.

- On each page, write: I am_____.

- Help your child to write the word using the techniques from above. Read the pattern book.

- Take photos of family members. Make a book. Glue a photo on each page.

- On each page, write: Here is_____.

- Help your child write: Mom, Dad, and siblings' names.

- Read it! To everyone! Grandma, Grandpa, the dog.

# BEGIN TO WRITE

It's important to build up a bank of sight words. It makes writing easier. It'll make reading easier, too. Your child will recognize words in reading that they learn to write.

## Give your child a reason to write:
- A note or letter to a grandparent/mom/dad/sibling/dog
- A shopping list
- A to-do list
- A home-made greeting card for a relative or friend
- A menu for a special meal
- Signs for a playhouse
- Labels for objects around the house – door, bathroom, dog food, my room

## Working on Sight Words During Story Writing
- An excellent way to learn a new sight word is to need it for a story your child is trying to write. It becomes a meaningful activity.
- Let's use this as an example: "The dog is jumping." Practise the word "is". A very handy sight word to know.
- On a little whiteboard, at the top, place the magnetic letters for "is" . Make sure both are lower case letters.
- Then, ask your child to copy the word right under those letters with a marker. Do it three times.
- Then, erase the words. Cover up the magnetic letters with your hand and ask your child to write "is".
- If you child doesn't remember the letters, uncover the magnetic letters for a look.

# BEGIN TO WRITE

- Have your child copy it again a couple of times, then, cover it up again.
- Do one new sight word a day or every couple of days.
- Review the sight words.

## Sight Words on a Ring

- Remember the ring of sight words that you made with your child. The next time your child is writing a sentence with any of the learned sight words, remind them that they know how to read that word – *show it to them*.

- You can also have some level A and B books that your child read and knows (or even memorized) handy to show your child. Point out the sight word that they could read – now they can write it!

- If need be, quickly make the word with magnetic letters. • Practise writing the learned sight words every day on

- a whiteboard or a piece of paper.

- Use the **KINDERGARTEN SIGHT WORD LIST** as a reference (See Resources)

# WRITING TIPS

## WRITING SIGHT WORDS

Practise writing "word families". The last part of the word is the same.

If you teach 'sun' you can also teach 'fun'.
Do it in a column such as this. Have your child write the word under the word at the top. sun fun bun run.

**Try these:**

| c/at | s/it | h/op | w/ill |
|------|------|------|-------|
| b/at | h/it | p/op | p/ill |
| h/at | b/it | t/op | h/ill |
| p/at | l/it | m/op | m/ill |

**Say:**
If you can write the word 'cat', how would you write 'bat'?

What would you change the 'c' to? (Say the 'b' sound)

How would you write 'mat', 'hat', 'pat'? (Say the first sound)

All you do is change the first letter! This is easily done with magnetic letters.

# WRITING TIPS

## WRITING LETTERS

**There are many fun ways to learn to write the letters of alphabet.** There are 26 upper case and 26 lower case letters. That's a lot of letters! Teach the letters one at a time and a good place to begin is with the letters of your child's name because they are the most meaningful.

### Teach one letter at a time.

- Teach one letter a day, or every several days depending on how ready your child is.

- Start with an upper case or capital letter, then once that is learned, move on to the lower case or small letter

- Give your child blank, white, unlined paper. Your child doesn't have the fine motor control yet to stay between the lines. Use a little whiteboard or blackboard.

- Ask what sound the letter makes.

### Trace the letter.

- Begin by printing a letter your child can trace, one with broken lines.

- Make the letter at least about 1 to 2 inches tall so it's easier for your child to form.

- Your child can use a marker or a chunky pencil to trace the letter.

- You can also print a letter with a highlighter, your child traces over it with a darker coloured marker.

## WRITING LETTERS

## Copy the letter.
- Once your child can trace letters easily, move on to having them copy the letter that you print
- Make the letters about 1 to 2 inches tall. Continue to use unlined paper.

## Play a game.
- "Write" a big letter on your child's back with your finger tip. Can they guess it? Can they guess what it is? Have your child "write" a letter on your back. Guess!

# WRITING TIPS

## WRITING NAMES

**The first word your child will likely write will be their name.** It's personal. It has special meaning. It's a very good place to start. When your child is ready to write their name will vary, but most children will be able to try around age 3 or 4. It takes time for the little muscles in your child's hands to develop to the point where they are able to hold a pencil or crayon and have enough control to form letters. It's called fine motor control.

### Make a name card for your child.

- Use a piece of white card stock or bristol board about 8 inches by 4 inches.

- Print the name using a dark marker.

- The first letter is a capital and the rest of the letters are lower case.

- This is the way of convention and it is the way a kindergarten teacher will teach your child to write his or her name. So, do it this way. That way your child won't have to unlearn it.

- If you have a laminator, laminate the card, if not, use clear tape for a do-it-yourself job. Keep the card in your writing centre for quick reference.

### Teach your child how to copy the name.

- Give your child a piece of blank, white paper. Unlined.

# WRITING NAMES

- At this stage, children don't have the fine motor control needed to stay between the lines.
- Show your child how to print each letter.
- Use verbal directions while you're doing it. For example, if the first letter is an 'A', while printing it, say - Down, down, across. If it's a 'B', say - Down, around and around, and so on.
- Practise every day.
- Your child can sign greeting cards for relatives and friends.

## Trace the name.

- Make a tracing name card.
- If your child is having difficulty doing this or needs more practice, make another card but print the letters in broken lines for your child to trace. Laminate the card and have your child use a dry-erase marker so the card can be used over and over again. Show your child how to trace the letters with the same verbal directions. Practise every day.

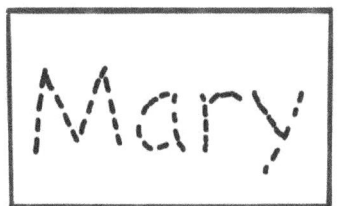

## Write the name in the air.

- Show your child how to write his or her name in the air with big arm movements. Use verbal directions - "Down, around and down!" for an "R".

# WRITING NAMES

## Same name different ways.

- Make your child's name in different ways.
- Have fun making your child's name with glitter glue, beans, pasta, fruity cereal, jelly beans, yarn, etc. (Watch out for swallowing hazards.)
- Make a name card out of card stock or bristol board.
- Your child can write the name with a black marker in big letters, or if not, you can write it.
- Have your child glue the items onto the letters. Post the artwork on a wall.
- Use playdough to form the letters. Make the name with magnetic letters on the refrigerator.
- Use sidewalk chalk on the driveway.
- Use a big brush and water on the driveway. Use soap paint on bathroom tiles.

Good luck! Remember to have fun with your child and give lots of praise.

Each child develops at their own rate. Most children will be ready to read and write successfully if you do these pre-reading activities.

# RESOURCES

## BOOKS, LINKS, AND MUSIC

## BOOKS:

LEVELED BOOKS - SUPER HAMMY BOOKS - DC CANADA EDUCATION PUBLISHING - also French

My Super Hammy books can be purchased as a set or individually and are very affordable!

SUPER HAMMY ABC BOOK - also French

SUPER HAMMY BOOKS-AMAZON.CA

LEVELED BOOKS - BLUEBERRY HILL BOOKS

LEVELLED BOOKS - READINGREADINGBOOKS.COM

LEVELLED BOOKS – READING A-Z.COM

CANADIAN CHILDREN'S BOOK CENTRE

100 BEST CHILDREN'S PICTURE BOOKS

100 BEST BOOKS FOR CHILDREN - BOOK TRUST.ORG.U.K.

## USEFUL LINKS:

www.readwritethink.org

www.colorincolorado.org - Tips for Parents

Reading and Writing with Your Child - Ontario Ministry of Education

Parents.education.govt.nz

Starfall.com - phonics, reading

International Children's Digital Library -

Oxford Owl - 250 French books

## RESOURCES: BOOKS, LINKS, AND MUSIC

## MUSIC:

Raffi

Fred Penner

Sharon Lois and Bram

30 Traditional Nursery Rhymes

# PRINTABLES

## LINKS AND WORKSHEETS

To download and print these worksheets:
Go to www.oksannacrawleyauthor.com

You may also click on the links below:

LETTER NAMES TEST

LETTER SOUNDS TEST

ABC FISH TEMPLATE

KINDERGARTEN SIGHT WORD LIST

KINDERGARTEN SIGHT WORD FLASHCARDS

KINDERGARTEN SIGHT WORD TEST

GRADE ONE SIGHT WORDS

HOW BOOKS WORK CHECKLIST

WHAT TO SAY TO HELP YOUR CHILD READ

HOMEMADE PLAYDOUGH RECIPE

# PRINTABLES: LINKS AND WORKSHEETS

**Letter Names Test**

<u>Letter Names</u>

Point to each letter starting at A and go across to U. Ask your child to name the letter. Circle the letter if your child knows it.

| | | | | |
|---|---|---|---|---|
| A | F | K | P | U |
| B | G | L | Q | V |
| C | H | M | R | W |
| D | I | N | S | X |
| E | J | O | T | Y |
| Z | | | | |

| | | | | |
|---|---|---|---|---|
| a | f | k | p | u |
| b | g | l | q | v |
| c | h | m | r | w |
| d | i | n | s | x |
| e | j | o | t | y |
| z | | | | |

# PRINTABLES: LINKS AND WORKSHEETS

**Letter Sounds Test**

<u>Letter Sounds</u>

Point to each letter starting at A and go across to U. Ask your child what sound the letter makes. Circle the letter if your child knows the sound.

| | | | | |
|---|---|---|---|---|
| A | F | K | P | U |
| B | G | L | Q | V |
| C | H | M | R | W |
| D | I | N | S | X |
| E | J | O | T | Y |
| Z | | | | |

| | | | | |
|---|---|---|---|---|
| a | f | k | p | u |
| b | g | l | q | v |
| c | h | m | r | w |
| d | i | n | s | x |
| e | j | o | t | y |

## PRINTABLES: LINKS AND WORKSHEETS

**ABC Fish Template**

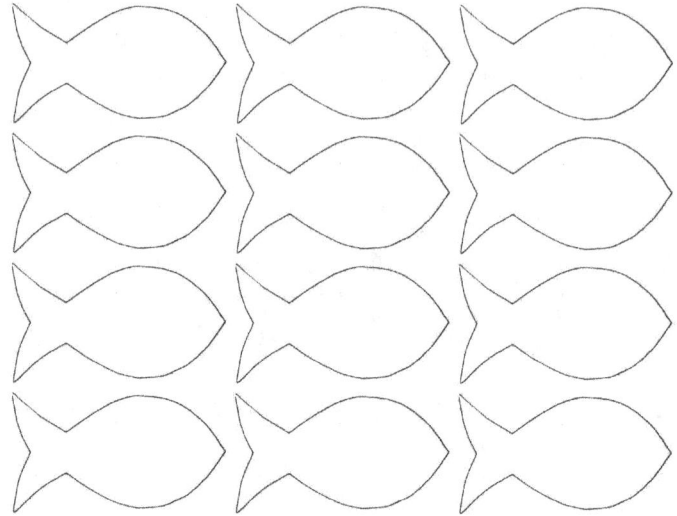

# PRINTABLES: LINKS AND WORKSHEETS

**Kindergarten Sight Word List**

<u>Kindergarten Sight Word List</u>

| I  | it | he | can | look |
|----|----|----|-----|------|
| a  | to | do | and | here |
| am | is | me | the | said |
| an | no | go | see | like |
| at | so | we | you | come |
| up | in | my | red | down |

-adapted from Fountas & Pinnell

PRINTABLES: LINKS AND WORKSHEETS

**Kindergarten Sight Word Flashcards**

| a | and |
|---|---|
| am | at |
| an | up |

| can | come |
|---|---|
| do | down |
| you | we |

| | |
|---|---|
| red | see |
| so | the |
| to | said |

| | |
|---|---|
| it | like |
| me | my |
| no | look |

PRINTABLES: LINKS AND WORKSHEETS

| go | he |
|---|---|
| I | in |
| is | here |

# PRINTABLES: LINKS AND WORKSHEETS

## Kindergarten Sight Word Test

### Kindergarten Sight Word Assessment

Ask your child to read the sight words one column at a time starting with the first column on the left.
Cover up the other columns with a piece of paper.
Circle the word if your child knows it.

| I  | it | he | can | look |
|----|----|----|-----|------|
| a  | to | do | and | here |
| am | is | me | the | said |
| an | no | go | see | like |
| at | so | we | you | come |
| up | in | my | red | down |

-adapted from Fountas & Pinnell

# PRINTABLES: LINKS AND WORKSHEETS

## Grade One Sight Words

### Grade One Sight Words

| | | | | |
|---|---|---|---|---|
| all | came | how | or | us |
| are | did | if | out | very |
| as | from | into | put | was |
| away | get | little | play | went |
| back | going | make | saw | what |
| be | had | make | she | where |
| because | has | not | that | who |
| been | have | now | they | will |
| but | her | of | this | with |
| by | him | one | two | your |

-Fountas & Pinnell

# PRINTABLES: LINKS AND WORKSHEETS

**How Books Work**

### How Books Work Checklist

- front of the book
- title
- where do we start reading
- which way do we go
- one-to-one matching
- a letter
- a word
- the first letter of a word
- the last letter of a word
- an upper case letter (capital)
- a lower case letter (small letter)
- a period
- a question mark
- quotation marks (talking marks)

# PRINTABLES: LINKS AND WORKSHEETS

## What to Say to Your Child to Help Them Read

**READING PROMPTS**

PROMPTS TO USE WHEN YOUR CHILD IS TRYING TO FIGURE OUT A WORD IN A SENTENCE. START WITH NUMBR 1 OR 2 ALWAYS.

1. LOOK AT THE PICTURE FOR CLUES. WHAT WORD WOULD MAKE SENSE?
2. TRY A WORD THAT MAKES SENSE.
3. TRY A WORD. DOES THAT SOUND RIGHT? DO WE TALK LIKE THAT?
4. TRY A WORD. YOU SAID_____. CHECK THE WORD WITH YOUR FINGER. ARE ALL THE LETTERS THERE FOR THE SOUNDS YOU MADE?
5. SAY THE FIRST SOUND OF THE WORD. WHAT WOULD MAKE SENSE?
6. GO BACK TO THE BEGINNING OF THE SENTENCE, RE-READ AND SAY THE FIRST SOUND OF THE WORD YOU'RE TRYING TO FIGURE OUT? WHAT WOULD MAKE SENSE?
7. RUN YOUR FINGER UNDER THE WORD AND SAY THE SOUNDS SLOWLY. WHAT WORD WOULD MAKE SENSE?
8. IF YOUR CHILD CAN'T FIGURE IT OUT, GIVE IT TO THEM.

PRAISE YOUR CHILD!

PRINTABLES: LINKS AND WORKSHEETS

## HOMEMADE PLAYDOUGH

This is a recipe that I used to make playdough for my kindergarten classes and for my own kids.

- 2 cups all-purpose flour
- 3/4 cup salt
- 2 cups lukewarm water
- 2 Tablespoons vegetable oil

For colour: You can add food colouring of your choice. If your child has allergies to dye, you can use natural dyes such as beet powder or turmeric. You can also add glitter for some extra fun!

You can also add 4 tsp. of cream of tartar but it's not necessary. It acts as a bit more of a preservative but the salt does that, too.

## INSTRUCTIONS

- Mix the flour and salt together in a large pot.
- Add the water and oil.
- Add the colouring if using.
- Cook over medium heat and stir constantly.
- The dough will begin to form a ball.
- Remove from heat and put in bowl. Let cool for a bit.
- Knead the dough.
- Store in a plastic bag or container with a lid.
- It lasts a long time but eventually dries out. If it gets moldy, throw it out!

DO NOT EAT! KEEP AWAY FROM DOGS (PETS) BECAUSE OF THE SALT.

# ACKNOWLEDGEMENTS

Many thanks to Mrs. McCabe's Kindergarten Class at St. John Fisher School for examples of children's writing and drawings.

Thank you to my proof reader – Larissa, the best daughter anyone could have.

> How do you spell 'love'?
> – Piglet
> You don't spell it...you feel it.
> – Pooh
>
> A.A. Milne
> (Winnie the Pooh)

# BIBLIOGRAPHY

Clay, M. *Literacy Lessons: Designed for Individuals, Part One: Why? When? and How?*. Portsmouth, NH: Heinemann, 2005

Clay, M. *Literacy Lessons: Designed for Individuals, Part Two: Teaching Procedures*. Portsmouth, NH: Heinemann, 2005

Fountas, I. Pinnell, G. *The Fountas & Pinnell Literacy Continuum: A Tool for Assessment, Planning, and Teaching, PreK-8*. Portsmouth, NH: Heinemann, 2016

Fountas, I. Pinnell, G. *The Fountas and Pinnell Prompting Guide 1(A Tool for Literacy Teachers, Grades K-2)*. Portsmouth, NH: Heinemann, 2007

Images: Pixabay unless otherwise stated
Images: pgs. 8,13, 30, 31, 58, 59: O. Crawley
All printables: O. Crawley (for personal use only)

## ABOUT THE AUTHOR

Oksanna Crawley is the author and illustrator of the *Super Hammy — My First Reading Series*, a collection of 30 levelled books recommended by *Professionally Speaking*, journal of the Ontario College of Teachers. Crawley has 25 years teaching experience as a kindergarten teacher, a reading specialist in early literacy and an English as a Second Language teacher. She has a passion for helping children learn to read and write.

Website: https://oksannacrawleyauthor.com

www.ingramcontent.com/pod-product-compliance
Lightning Source LLC
Chambersburg PA
CBHW072103290426
44110CB00014B/1805